GETTING INTO NATURE™

GETTING INTO NATURE™

Oak Trees

INSIDE AND OUT

Text by Andrew Hipp
Illustrations by Fiammetta Dogi

The Rosen Publishing Group's
PowerKids Press™
New York

Published in 2004 in North America
by The Rosen Publishing Group, Inc.
29 East 21st Street, New York, NY 10010

Book Design:
Andrea Dué s.r.l., Florence, Italy

Illustrations:
Fiammetta Dogi and Studio Stalio
Map by Alessandro Bartolozzi

Scientific advice for botanical illustrations:
Riccardo Maria Baldini

Library of Congress Cataloging-in-Publication Data
Hipp, Andrew.
Oak trees inside and out / by Andrew Hipp.
   p. cm. — (Getting into nature)
Summary: Discusses what a valuable resource oak trees are and
describes their various parts, including roots, trunks, leaves,
flowers, and acorns.
Includes bibliographical references (p.   ) and index.
ISBN 0-8239-4206-6 (library binding)
1. Oak—Juvenile literature. [1. Oak. 2. Trees.] I. Title. II. Series.
SD397.012H56 2004
634.9'721—dc22
                                                        2003015533

Manufactured in Italy by Eurolitho S.p.A., Milan

Contents

Oaks

Oak trees are built strong, allowing them to live for hundreds of years. **Tannic acids** in the leaves and bark guard oaks from **fungi** and insects. Oak trunks, the trees' thick main stems, store water for use during dry periods. Oaks send up new sprouts from their roots if they are burned down or eaten by animals. Many oaks have thick bark that protects them from fire. For these reasons, oaks are among the most important **species** in many forests, woodlands, and other **ecosystems**.

Oaks are important in many societies. In some parts of the world, people grow coppices, or small forests, of oak trees that they harvest, or gather, as a crop. They cut down the young trees every 15 to 30 years and use the wood for fires to heat their homes and cook food. The harvested oaks, which have stored energy, or strength, down in their roots, sprout again and form many new, thin branches.

5

Oaks of the World

Oak trees most likely **evolved** in North America, Europe, and Asia between 40 million and 60 million years ago. The first oaks were probably European and Asian, but most species evolved from North American oaks whose acorns were carried across a land bridge that once connected North America and Asia more than 15 million years ago.

Most of us know oaks as trees found in forests where the weather is not too hot or cold, such as in North America and Europe. Many oaks, however, grow as trees or **shrubs** in **tropical** areas of the world, too. Around 140 species grow in Mexico alone. Although many North American and European oaks drop leaves during cold or dry seasons, tropical oaks keep their leaves year-round.

Leaves and acorns of the English oak (*Quercus robur*)

THE RANGE AND SPREAD OF OAKS

EUROPE

ASIA

AFRICA

S. AMERICA

AUSTRALIA

Leaves and acorns of the
Downy oak (*Quercus pubescens*)

The Oak's Roots and Shoots

Roots keep oaks secured to the ground. The youngest parts of the root system are near the tips of the roots. They are covered with root hairs and fungi, which allow the roots to collect water and **nutrients**. Older parts of the root system are woody and covered with bark. Woody roots connect to the shoot system, which is made of the trunk, branches, leaves, and flowers—all the parts of a tree that are above the ground.

Bottom, left to right: These drawings show the growth of a sessile oak (*Quercus petraea*) and its roots from seedling to young tree.

The root is the first part of the oak tree to come out of an acorn. It may grow more than 1.5 feet (0.5 meters) into the ground in less than a year, guided downward by cells in the root tip that

One-year-old sapling

acorn

side roots

taproot

feeder roots

Oak seedling

Right: Oak roots are wrapped by the rootlike growths of fungi such as pore mushrooms. Fungi collect a nutrient called phosphorus from the soil, which they trade to oaks in return for carbon. In this way, both mushrooms and oaks get what they need to grow.

respond to the force of weight. As the plant grows older, this taproot produces side roots that grow as much as 45 feet (14 meters) outwards. Feeder roots grow off of the side roots. Some grow upward into the very rich soil right near the surface. Others grow downward in search of water and **minerals**. Oaks that live in dry places can form root systems more than 25 feet (7.6 meters) deep.

Young oak tree

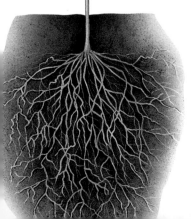

Pore mushrooms
(*Boletus edulis*)

The Oak's Trunk

The wood that makes up an oak trunk contains sapwood and heartwood. Sapwood carries water and minerals from roots to the leaves. Heartwood stores waste produced by the tree. Wrapped around the wood is inner bark, which carries food from the leaves to the rest of the tree, and dead

Below left: This drawing shows the inside of an oak's trunk.

Heartwood. Wood that no longer carries water, housing only dead cells.

Pith. Tissue, or matter, at the center of a shoot.

Ray. Stores water and nutrients and moves them from the edge of the trunk to the center.

Sapwood. Water-carrying wood, housing living cells, dead fibers, and water-carrying vessels.

Outer bark (dead).

Inner bark (alive). Living tissue that carries sugars from leaves to the trunk and roots.

Vascular cambium. A single layer of cells that each year produces new sapwood and new inner bark.

outer bark, which protects the trunk from fire and other damage. Between the inner bark and the sapwood is a thin level of cells called the vascular cambium.

Each year, the vascular cambium produces a layer of sapwood and a layer of inner bark. In many oaks, the first sapwood produced in the spring has very wide vessels, or water-carrying tubes. These vessels carry large amounts of water from the heavy spring rains. Vessels produced in summer and fall are much narrower. This difference in the thickness of vessels creates annual, or yearly, growth rings, which we can count to learn a tree's age.

From Wood to Lumber

Oak wood is made mostly of strong fibers and water-carrying vessels. Vessels start out as living cells that form thick, tough walls. Vessels soon die and become hollow, like straws. They connect end-to-end to move water and minerals from the tips of the roots to every leaf on the tree. In white oaks and their relatives, the oldest vessels become blocked with balloonlike growths called tyloses, which prevent the vessels from carrying water. Tyloses also prevent sicknesses from spreading through old vessels. Oaks that produce tyloses provide the best wood for making kegs and sailing ships, because tyloses help keep water from dripping through the wood.

The oak's vessels and fiber cells give the wood its great strength. Because oaks grow very slowly, oak forests take a long time to grow back after they are cut down.

Left and above: Because oak is a dense, or thick, strong wood, it is often used to build houses and furniture.

Above right: These drawings show the different ways oak trunks can be cut to make planks for use in home and furniture construction.

Right: This is a stove that makes heat by burning wood. Because oak wood is so dense, it burns for a long time and gives off a lot of heat. Oaks have provided people with firewood for many centuries, helping them live through even the coldest winters.

Oak Leaves

All living things are made partly of **carbon**. People and other animals get their carbon from food. Some of the carbon we eat gets turned into a gas called carbon dioxide. The carbon dioxide leaves our body when we breathe out. Green plants, such as oak trees, get their carbon from the carbon dioxide that we and other living things breathe out.

Carbon dioxide enters oak leaves through tiny pores, or holes, called stomata. Inside the leaf, matter called **chlorophyll** combines carbon dioxide with water. Chlorophyll uses power from sunlight to turn the carbon dioxide and water into sugar and **oxygen** in an action called **photosynthesis**. The sugar that an oak leaf makes gets turned into wood, bark, flowers, leaves, and acorns. The oxygen is released from the leaves and breathed by people and animals.

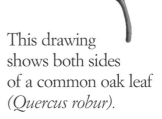

This drawing shows both sides of a common oak leaf (*Quercus robur*).

1. This is an oak leaf seen from the inside. At top and bottom are the epidermal, or surface, layers of the leaf. Sandwiched between them are mesophyll cells, in which photosynthesis takes place.

2. This is a mesophyll cell. In it are chloroplasts, the part of the cell where photosynthesis takes place. The vacuole is the part of the cell that stores air or liquid. The nucleus is the center around which the cell grows. It tells the cell how to do its work.

3. This is a close-up of a chloroplast. The green objects are called grana (seen in close-up below). They are made up of individually stacked thylakoids. Thylakoids are membranes, or thin sheets, that control the movement of sugar and water into and out of the chloroplast, helping photosynthesis to take place.

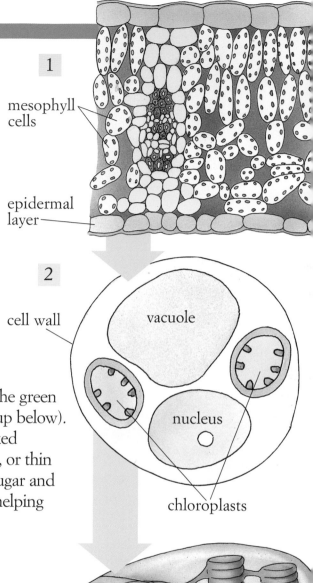

1

mesophyll cells

epidermal layer

2

cell wall

vacuole

nucleus

chloroplasts

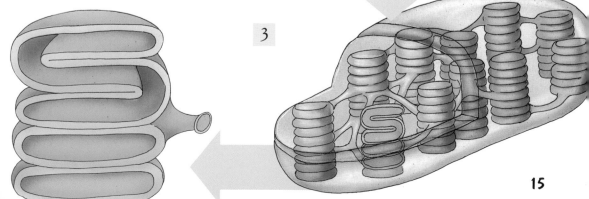

3

Oak Flowers

Oaks produce male, or boy, flowers and female, or girl, flowers. Male flowers hang on long, threadlike **catkins** and produce huge amounts of **pollen**.

On windy days early in the growing season, clouds of pollen blow from the male flowers to the open stigmas of female flowers. Stigmas stick out of a flower and catch pollen. After a pollen grain lands, the stigma sends a message that causes the pollen grain to grow a long, narrow pollen tube. This tube snakes down into the female flower and **fertilizes** the **ovules** inside.

Above:
Flowering
turkey oak
(Quercus cerris)

Each female oak flower holds six ovules. Usually only one ovule ripens to become a seed. The other five ovules die off.

Many oaks form male flowers high on the tree, where wind will catch the pollen and carry it farthest. Female flowers are often spread on new branches all over the tree.

You can tell where the female flowers have been by looking for the acorns they make.

Left: Female flower of a scrub oak

Top: Male flower of a scrub oak, with growing anthers

female flower

catkins

male flower

Left: Flowering scrub oak (*Quercus ilicifolia*)

17

Acorns

Cork oak
(*Quercus suber*)

Acorn

acorn cap

seed leaves
(cotyledons)

acorn shell

Acorns are nuts
produced only by oaks.
Inside each acorn are two
seed leaves that fit together
like two halves of a ball. These seed leaves
hold food stored by the mother tree. Stuffed
between the seed leaves is the baby plant.
A hard shell and a cap guard the seed.

When acorns **germinate**, they grow and
begin to sprout, and their seed leaves swell
and break the acorn wall. A root comes out
of the acorn and travels down through
the leaves, twisting around branches
to reach the soil. Soon, a shoot grows
up from the acorn. For the first two
years of life, an oak will get most of
its energy from the seed leaves. Most
seedlings are eaten in their first year
or die from lack of water or sunlight.

English oak
(*Quercus robur*)

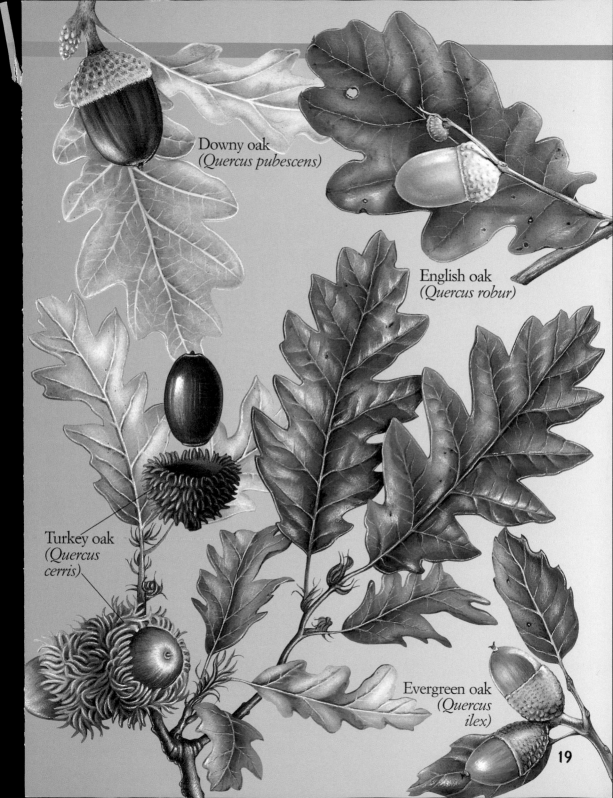

Downy oak
(Quercus pubescens)

English oak
(Quercus robur)

Turkey oak
*(Quercus
cerris)*

Evergreen oak
*(Quercus
ilex)*

19

Who Plants the Acorns?

Acorns are a favorite food of mice, deer, bears, chipmunks, squirrels, pigs, and such birds as turkeys, jays, wood pigeons, and acorn woodpeckers. Many acorns are eaten before they can grow. Others are hidden in holes in trees or dens found under the ground—places where acorns cannot grow into seedlings. A few animals, however, such as jays and squirrels, hide their seeds in holes in the ground that are not very deep. Jays and squirrels cannot eat all the acorns that they hide.

Eurasian jay
(*Garrulus glandarius*)

Bottom left:
Ever since pigs were first raised by humans, they have often been taken to oak groves to feed on acorns.

Grey squirrel
(*Sciurus carolinensis*)

By hiding these acorns to eat later, they plant oak trees all over the land. North American blue jays can carry as many as five acorns at a time in their throats. They bury many of these acorns to eat in winter. Jays are careful to collect only acorns that are not full of hungry insects. Insects can eat a pile of acorns before the jay gets a chance to enjoy them. Squirrels, too, are careful to store only acorns that will last through the winter. If a squirrel picks up an acorn that is full of insects, it will often eat the acorn right away, insects and all.

Above: An acorn woodpecker *(Melanerpes formicivorus)* hides its store of acorns in an oak's trunk.

Least chipmunk *(Tamias minimus)*

21

What Happened to the Passenger Pigeons?

Before 1900, North American passenger pigeons ate more oak acorns than any other animal. Like jays, they could carry acorns for many miles. Passenger pigeons were most likely very important in spreading oak trees. Unlike jays, passenger pigeons traveled in very large flocks. Flocks of passenger pigeons numbering in the tens of millions were occasionally reported to hide the sun like a large cloud, darkening the sky in midday. Passenger pigeons could clean an entire forest of acorns in only a few years.

Throughout the 1800s, hunters shipped millions of passenger pigeons each year to restaurants in the eastern United States. Hunters killed so many passenger pigeons that the huge flocks were reduced to a dozen birds. By 1900, the passenger pigeon no longer existed in the wild.

Passenger pigeons, like the one pictured at right, disappeared before scientists had a chance to study their life history closely. We may never know how important passenger pigeons might have been in planting the oak forests we see today.

The Sheltering Oak

Mistletoe

Oaks provide food and homes for many animals, including **gall**-making insects like cynipid wasps. These wasps of the Cynipidae family live off oaks. Gall makers place their eggs into oak buds, branches, or leaves. Matter from the egg or the **larva** that comes out of it causes the plant to swell up, forming a home for the insect.

Above:
Animals are not the only living things that depend on oaks for a home. One group of plants, the mistletoes, produce seeds that stick to oak branches. After the seeds germinate, mistletoe roots dig through the oak bark and into the branches, sucking water and minerals out of the tree.

Left: The oak fungus bitter panellus (*Panellus stipticus*) glows in the dark on moist fall evenings.

Gall-making insects may prefer oaks because the high levels of tannic acid in the tree guard young insects from other insects and fungi that might attack the gall makers.

Try to find an oak tree near your home that you can watch throughout the year. What birds visit the tree? What insects make their home in it? What fungi grow on it, and what plants grow beneath it? What crawls through the leaves that fall on the ground? You may find that your oak tree is home to more than you ever imagined.

Above: This is a marble gall produced by a cynipid wasp (*Andricus kollari*).

Right: Honey mushrooms (*Armillaria mellea*) grow on an oak's trunk and branches.

Glossary

carbon (KAR-bin) An element that is found in all living things and all natural unliving things.

catkins (KAT-kins) Strings or long bunches of tiny flowers.

chlorophyll (KLOR-uh-fill) The green matter in most plants that takes power from the sun to make plant food.

ecosystems (EE-koh-sis-tems) Groups of living things that live together in the same area, sharing and often fighting for food, water, air, and space.

evolved (ih-VAHLVD) Having grown and changed over time.

fertilizes (FUR-tih-lyz-iz) When a male seed causes the growth of new life by touching a female egg.

fungi (FUN-jeye) A group of many-celled living things that gather food from their surroundings, often from dead things or other living things.

gall (GAHL) A growth on a plant that is produced by an insect or other creature's egg laying.

germinate (JER-mi-nayt) To begin to grow from a seed.

larva (LAHR-vuh) An insect in its early life stage.

minerals (MIH-ner-ulz) Natural elements from the soil, many of which are needed by plants to stay healthy.

nutrients (NOO-tree-intz) Something that feeds living things and makes them healthy and strong.

ovules (OV-yulz) The matter inside a plant that grows up to become seeds.

oxygen (OK-sih-jen) A gas that is in air and water. People and animals need oxygen to breathe and keep their bodies running.

photosynthesis (foh-toh-SIN-thuh-sis) The action in which green plants use power from sunlight to turn carbon dioxide and water into sugar and oxygen.

pollen (PAH-lin) Tiny grains that carry a part of the material needed to produce a plant seed.

shrubs (SHRUBZ) Low, woody plants.

species (SPEE-sheez) A single kind of plant, animal, or other living thing.

tannic acids (TA-nik A-sidz) Liquid matter in plants that gives them strength.

tropical (TRAH-puh-kul) Areas of the world in which there is no frost and temperatures are warm enough to allow plants to grow year-round.

Index

Web Sites

Due to the changing nature of Internet links, PowerKids Press has developed an online list of Web sites related to the subject of this book. This site is updated regularly. Please use this link to access the list:

www.powerkidslinks.com/gin/oak

About the Author

Andrew Hipp has been working as a naturalist in Madison, Wisconsin, since 1993. He is currently finishing his doctoral work in botany at the University of Wisconsin. Andrew and his wife, Rachel Davis, are collaborating on an illustrated field guide to common sedges of Wisconsin as they look forward to the birth of their first child.

Acknowledgments
This book draws on the research and writing of M. D. Abrams, C. S. Adkisson, X. Chen, W. C. Johnson, G. Keator, R. Lewington, K. A. Longman, W. H. Lyford, P. S. Manos, K. C. Nixon, J. Price, T. S. Sharkey, P. Smallwood, M. Steele, G. N. Stone, A. R. Tiedemann, S. Yeh, and their collaborators. The author gratefully acknowledges Dr. R. J. Jensen for reviewing a draft of this manuscript.

Photo Credits